Dear Parent:
Your child's love of reading starts here!

Every child learns to read in a different way and at his or her own speed. Some go back and forth between reading levels and read favorite books again and again. Others read through each level in order. You can help your young reader improve and become more confident by encouraging his or her own interests and abilities. From books your child reads with you to the first books he or she reads alone, there are I Can Read Books for every stage of reading:

SHARED READING
Basic language, word repetition, and whimsical illustrations, ideal for sharing with your emergent reader

BEGINNING READING
Short sentences, familiar words, and simple concepts for children eager to read on their own

READING WITH HELP
Engaging stories, longer sentences, and language play for developing readers

READING ALONE
Complex plots, challenging vocabulary, and high-interest topics for the independent reader

ADVANCED READING
Short paragraphs, chapters, and excit̶ for the perfect bridge to chapter boo̶

I Can Read Books have introduced children to the joy of reading since 1957. Featuring award-winning authors and illustrators and a fabulous cast of beloved characters, I Can Read Books set the standard for beginning readers.

A lifetime of discovery begins with the magical words "I Can Read!"

Visit www.icanread.com for information
on enriching your child's reading experience.

*To the mothers and grandmothers who are reading this
book with little ones they love.
—J.B.*

The author would like to thank David Mizejewski, naturalist, the National
Wildlife Federation, for sharing his expertise.

The National Wildlife Federation and Ranger Rick contributors: Children's
Publication and Licensing Staff.

Ranger Rick: I Wish I Was an Elephant
The National Wildlife Federation. Copyright © 2018. All rights reserved.
Manufactured in U.S.A. No part of this book may be used or reproduced in any manner whatsoever without
written permission except in the case of brief quotations embodied in critical articles and reviews. For
information address HarperCollins Children's Books, a division of HarperCollins Publishers, 195 Broadway,
New York, NY 10007.
www.icanread.com
www.RangerRick.com

Library of Congress Control Number: 2017954077
ISBN 978-0-06-243214-8 (trade bdg.)—ISBN 978-0-06-243213-1 (pbk.)

Typography by Brenda E. Angelilli
19 20 21 22 LSCC 10 9 8 7 6 5 ❖ First Edition

I Can Read! BEGINNING READING 1

Ranger Rick®

I Wish I Was an Elephant

by Jennifer Bové

HARPER

An Imprint of HarperCollinsPublishers

What if you wished you were an elephant?

Then you became one!

Could you eat like an elephant?

Talk like an elephant?

Live in an elephant family?

And would you want to? Find out!

Where would you live?

Many elephants live in Africa
on grassy plains called savannas.
The sun shines for months at a time.
It is a hot and dry place.
Elephants move around the savanna.
They often walk for many miles
to find water and food.

What would your family be like?

An elephant family is called a herd.

It usually has around twenty members.

The leader of the herd is a wise
and strong mother elephant.

Most of the other herd members are
female elephants, called cows.

Young elephants live in the
herd, too.

They are called calves.

Adult male elephants, called bulls,
live apart from the herd.

A mother elephant has one calf around every five years.

The whole elephant herd is excited when a calf is born.

They gather around the calf to meet the new family member.

They use their trunks like hands to gently touch and pet the baby.

As an elephant calf grows bigger,
the other elephants in the herd
help take care of the calf.
Sisters and aunts love to babysit.
Babysitters play with the calf
and protect it from danger
while Mom is busy finding food.

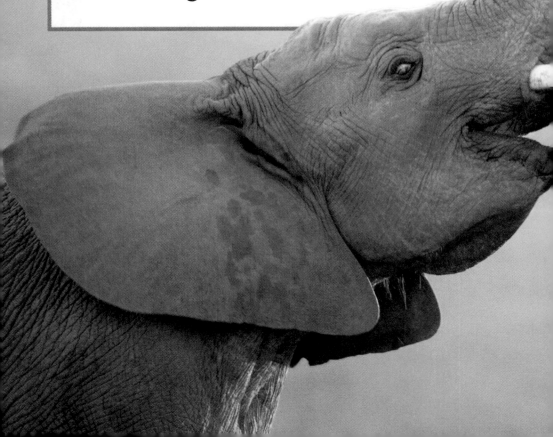

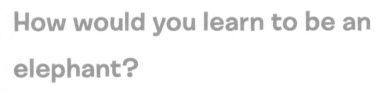

How would you learn to be an elephant?

Elephant calves learn from the herd. Older elephants show calves how to greet others by touching trunks and how to stick together when danger is near.

Calves learn that helping others
and working together
are important parts of herd life.

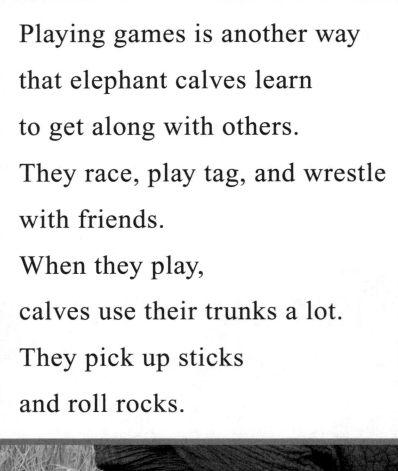

Playing games is another way
that elephant calves learn
to get along with others.
They race, play tag, and wrestle
with friends.
When they play,
calves use their trunks a lot.
They pick up sticks
and roll rocks.

What games do
you play with your
friends?

How would you talk?

Elephants make many sounds.
They can trumpet loudly to say,
"I'm excited!"

Adults roar to say, "Stay away!"
Elephants also talk by rumbling.
Rumbling is a low drumming sound
made in an elephant's throat.
Rumbles are hard for humans to hear,
but elephants can hear rumbles
from several miles away.

What would you eat?

Elephants eat leaves, grasses, and roots.

They like fruit and twigs, too.

Elephants find food by using their keen sense of smell.

They grasp food with their trunks and put it into their mouths.

Elephants need a lot of food, so they eat many times each day.

How would you wash up?

Elephants shower with their trunks.
They suck water into their trunks
and spray themselves.
They also spray one another for fun.

After washing, elephants roll in mud!
It sounds dirty,
but the mud dries on their skin
and protects them from bugs that bite.

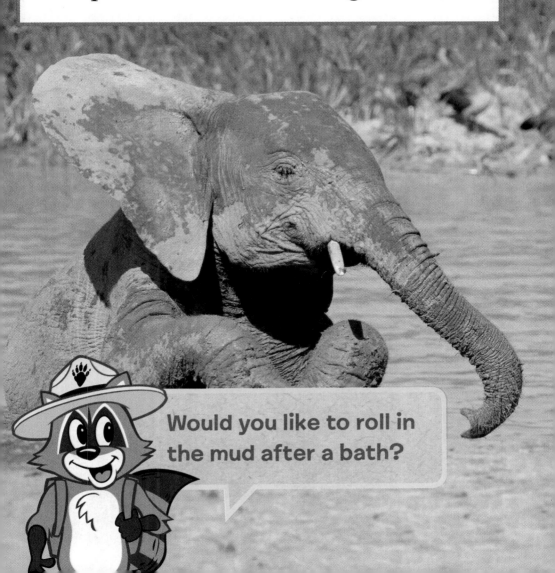

How would growing up change you?

Baby elephants get bigger every day. They grow long teeth called tusks. Elephants use them for digging roots and fighting predators, like lions.

When they are about
thirteen years old,
male elephants leave the herd.
Females stay with the herd for life.

Elephants can live up to sixty years—
a long time to grow and learn!
They are very intelligent
and have good memories.

Elephants can remember how to get to
water holes hundreds of miles away.
Elephants remember friends they met
long ago and trumpet happily
when they meet again.

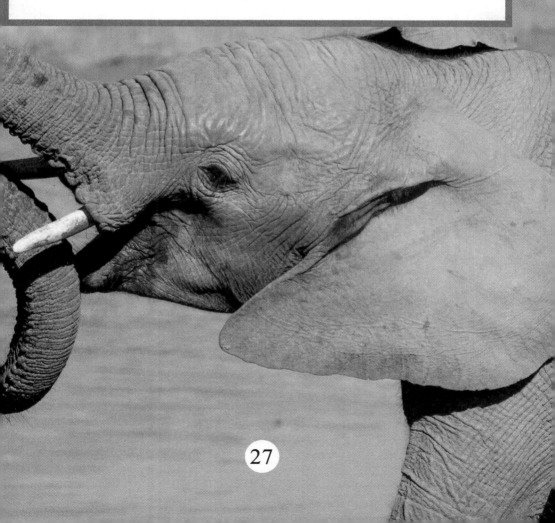

Being an elephant could be cool for a while.

But do you want to live in a hot, dry place?

Talk with rumbles?

Pick up things with your nose?

Luckily, you don't have to.

You're not an elephant.

You're YOU!

Did You Know?

🐾 The African elephant is the world's largest land animal.

🐾 Asian elephants are a little smaller than African elephants. They live in India, southern China, Indonesia, and a few other countries throughout Asia.

🐾 Elephants are good swimmers.

🐾 In zoos, elephants have learned to paint pictures and solve puzzles.

Elephant Soccer

Elephants use their trunks to do many things. Do you think elephants could play soccer with their trunks? Can you? Find out.

Gather five to ten players in a circle around a ball.

Players stand with legs apart and feet touching their neighbors' feet.

Players clasp their hands in front of them with arms straight to make elephant trunks.

Players bend down and try to hit the ball with their "trunks" so that it rolls through another player's legs.

Players also use their "trunks" to guard their own legs so that the ball does not pass through.

If the ball goes through a player's legs, then that player leaves the circle.

When only two players are left, they stand across from one another and try to hit the ball through the other's legs. The player who makes a goal wins.

Wild Words

Bull: an adult male elephant

Calf: a baby or young elephant

Cow: an adult female elephant

Herd: an elephant family

Predator: an animal that hunts and eats other animals; lions are predators that sometimes hunt young elephants

Savanna: a grassland with scattered shrubs and few trees

Trumpet: a loud noise made by elephants when excited, angry, or frightened

Trunk: an elephant's long nose that is used for smelling, drinking, bathing, trumpeting, grasping objects, and touching other elephants

Dig Deeper
WANT TO FIND OUT EVEN MORE ABOUT ELEPHANTS?

Check out the Ranger Rick website: www.RangerRick.com
SEARCH: elephants